The Ultimate Family
Christmas Cracker Advent Book

25 days of terrible jokes, pointless trivia
and more festive frivolity.

Jenny Kellett

BELLANOVA

MELBOURNE · SOFIA · BERLIN

The Ultimate Family Christmas Cracker Advent Book

Copyright © 2022 by Bellanova Books

www.bellanovabooks.com

All rights reserved. No part of this book may be reproduced in any form by any electronic or mechanical means including photocopying, recording, or information storage and retrieval without permission in writing from the author.

ISBN: 978-619-7695-49-6
Imprint: Bellanova Books

Ho-ho-hello!

Thanks for purchasing this book! In return, I guarantee that the next 25 days are going to be a **blast**.

This book is designed to be family-friendly, with a carefully crafted blend of activities, trivia and jokes that all age groups can enjoy.

If you enjoy the book, please consider leaving a **review**. As an independent author, it really makes a difference!

And most importantly, have a **wonderful holiday season!**

ON THIS DAY

1959 The Antarctic Treaty was signed by 12 countries.

Pablo Escobar, Bette Midler and Woody Allen were all born on **December 1.**

DID YOU KNOW?!

The **tallest** Christmas tree on display was in Seattle, USA. It measured 221 ft. (67 m) tall.

What do you call people who are afraid of Santa Claus?

— *Claustrophobic!*

QUIZ TIME!

1. What is a tree with fake snow called?

2. What is the name of the most popular red Christmas plant?

3. Which famous fairy tale inspired the first gingerbread houses?

ON THIS DAY

1983 The music video for Michael Jackson's *Thriller* aired on MTV.

Britney Spears, Gianni Versace and Aaron Rodgers were all born on **December 2.**

DID YOU KNOW?!

In Ukraine, **spiders** are considered symbols of luck at Christmas.

Who says 'oh-oh-oh'?

— Santa walking backwards!

QUIZ TIME!

1. What was the first name of Scrooge in *The Christmas Carol*?

2. What real-life store is the movie *Miracle on 34th Street* based on?

3. What is given on the seventh day of the song *Twelve Days of Christmas*?

Festive Food

Can you find all the Christmas food words below in the word search puzzle on the right?!

EGGNOG

TURKEY

MINCE PIES

GINGERBREAD

FRUITCAKE

TRIFLE

CANDY CANE

TANGERINE

SUGARPLUMS

COOKIES

STUFFING

```
W E D S S T U F F I N G F
Q E G G N O G N B V X E D
W R I V H G F S Y T R S W
C A N D Y C A N E B G U P
O E G F D S Q W D C F G O
O F E M K S D E F U D A I
K F R U I T C A K E S R U
I D B T E S R C N Y E P T
E S R H U D E I V T S L R
S A E V H R D E F A W U E
E W A V C X K Q G L N M F
W E D M I N C E P I E S B
V K H A D F A D Y U Y R V
D T A N G E R I N E W D C
```

ON THIS DAY

1967 The first human heart transplant was performed.

Andy Williams, Ozzy Osbourne and Julianne Moore were all born on **December 3.**

DID YOU KNOW?!

If you bought all of the gifts listed on **Twelve Days of Christmas** it would equal 364 presents.

What did the reindeer say when he saw an elf?

— Nothing. Reindeers can't talk!

QUIZ TIME!

1. What is Frosty the Snowman's nose made out of?

2. What Christmas drink is also known as 'milk punch'?

3. Where was Jesus born?

ON THIS DAY

1791   The world's oldest Sunday newspaper, **The Observer**, was first published in Britain.

Crazy Horse, Jay-Z and Tyra Banks were all born on **December 4**.

DID YOU KNOW?!

The first artificial Christmas trees were made from **goose feathers** dyed green. They were displayed in Germany around 1865.

How do you know when Santa is in the room?

— *You can sense his presents!*

QUIZ TIME!

1. When was the first Christmas card sent?

2. Which action film is a popular holiday film?

3. In which modern-day country was St Nicholas born?

Georgina the Gingerbread lady wants her **present**! Can you help her get to it?

ON THIS DAY

1933 — Prohibition ended in the United States.

Walt Disney, Martin van Buren and Ronnie O'Sullivan were all born on **December 5.**

DID YOU KNOW?!

Brenda Lee was only 13 years old when she recorded the original **Rockin' Around the Christmas Tree** in 1958.

What is the difference between the Christmas alphabet and the normal alphabet?

— *The Christmas one has no L (Noel).*

QUIZ TIME!

1. In *Polar Express*, which actor played six different roles?

2. Which country did eggnog come from?

3. In the movie *A Christmas Story*, what was Ralphie's little brother's name?

ON THIS DAY

2006 NASA released photos suggesting there could be liquid water on Mars.

Joyce Kilmer, Ira Gershwin and Agnes Moorehead were all born on **December 6.**

DID YOU KNOW?!

The idea of leaving cookies and milk for Santa Claus came from the Dutch, who would leave him food on **St. Nicholas' Feast Day**, December 6, in return for the presents he would leave.

Which of Santa's reindeers has bad manners?

— *Rude-olph!*

QUIZ TIME!

1. What was the first rule of The Code of Elves in the movie *Elf*?

2. What was the highest-grossing Christmas movie of all time?

3. How do you say "Merry Christmas" in Spanish?

Christmas
Colouring Challenge

Use the picture for inspiration, or create your own jolly masterpiece!

ON THIS DAY

1941   Pearl Harbour was attacked by the Japanese.

Larry Bird, Ellen Burstyn and Johnny Bench were all born on **December 7**.

DID YOU KNOW?!

Tinsel was invented in Germany in 1610. It was originally spun from real **silver**.

What do you call an elf who sings?

— *A wrapper!*

QUIZ TIME!

1. Which three of Santa's reindeers begin with the letter "D"?

2. Which popular Christmas song was actually written for Thanksgiving?

3. How does Buddy get to the North Pole in the movie *Elf*?

ON THIS DAY

1813 — Beethoven premiered his 7th Symphony in A in Vienna.

Jim Morrison, Nicki Minaj and Sinead O'Connor were all born on **December 8.**

DID YOU KNOW?!

The iconic Christmas tree in **London's Trafalgar Square** is an annual gift from Norway in gratitude of Britain's help during World War II.

What is the most popular Christmas carol in the desert?

— *Camel ye faithful.*

QUIZ TIME!

1. In which country did the Christmas tree tradition start?

2. In the song *Last Christmas*, who does WHAM! give their heart to?

3. Which well-known store made the world's largest ever gingerbread man?

Feeling Merry & Musical

Fill in the blanks from these famous Christmas songs. Name the song for bonus points!

1. The stars in the sky looked ___ ___ ___

2. Snowing ___ ___ up bushels of fun

3. It doesn't show signs of stopping,
   And I've bought some ___ for popping

4 Faithful friends who are dear to us
to gather ___ ___ ___ once more

5 With a corn cob ___ and a button ___, And
two eyes made out of ___

6 He knows if you've been ___ ___ ___,
So be good for goodness sake!

7 Silent night, holy ___!
___ quake at the sight.

8 Let the Christmas spirit ring
Later we'll have some
___ pie

ON THIS DAY

1979 — Smallpox was declared eradicated by the World Health Organisation.

Judi Dench, Kirk Douglas and John Milton were all born on **December 9.**

DID YOU KNOW?!

The Germanic word for 'mistletoe' means "**dung on a twig**". It comes from the mistle thrush bird, which eats the berries from the plant and then the digested droppings help germinate new plants.

Why would you invite a mushroom to a Christmas party?

— *Because he's a fun guy!*

QUIZ TIME!

1. What is mulled wine made of?

2. In which country do many people celebrate Christmas at the beach?

3. What type of bird often appears on Christmas cards?

ON THIS DAY

1768 — *Encyclopaedia Britannica* was first published.

Ada Lovelace, Emily Dickinson and George Shaw were all born on **December 10**.

DID YOU KNOW?!

Around 85% of Americans celebrate Christmas, but only 51% attend a Christmas church service.

What would a reindeer do if it lost its tail?

— *Go to a re-tail store!*

QUIZ TIME!

1. Which reindeer is named after Thunder?

2. What is the name of Rudolph the Red-Nosed Reindeer's son?

3. What does Santa's belly shake like?

ABC's

Can you think of a Christmas-related word beginning with each letter of the alphabet? Write it down or say it out loud. Keep going until someone can't think of anything. The person who keeps going the longest, wins!

A _____
B _____
C _____
D _____
E _____
F _____
G _____
H _____
I _____
J _____

K
L
M
N
O
P
Q
R
S
T
U
V
W
X
Y
Z

ON THIS DAY

1936 King Edward VIII abdicated from the British throne to marry American divorceé Wallis Simpson.

Hailee Steinfeld, Robert Koch and Rita Moreno were all born on **December 11.**

DID YOU KNOW?!

In Canada, Santa Claus has his own postcode, **HOH OHO**, where children can send their letters to Santa.

What is a female elf called?

— *A shelf.*

QUIZ TIME!

1. What is traditionally left out for Santa on Christmas Eve?

2. What day do the Spanish celebrate Christmas?

3. How many times does Santa check his list before he makes a delivery?

ON THIS DAY

1977 The movie *Saturday Night Fever* premiered.

Edvard Munch, Bob Barker and Frank Sinatra were all born on **December 12.**

DID YOU KNOW?!

Black Friday is not the **busiest shopping day** of the year: the two days right before Christmas are.

What do snowmen eat for lunch?

— *Icebergers!*

QUIZ TIME!

1. In *Home Alone*, where do Kevin's parents go when they leave him behind?

2. Which actor plays the Grinch in *How The Grinch Stole Christmas*?

3. In which country did the "Boxing Day" tradition originate?

Reindeer Games

Can you find all of Santa's reindeers in the word search puzzle on the right?!

- DASHER
- DANCER
- PRANCER
- VIXEN
- COMET
- DONNER
- BLITZER
- RUDOLPH
- CUPID

Y	T	R	E	F	D	S	V	B	G	F	D	S
U	B	L	I	T	Z	E	R	M	G	S	V	U
Y	V	G	F	D	P	U	Y	R	S	G	I	T
B	D	A	S	H	E	R	M	J	D	F	X	R
R	G	J	S	R	G	F	D	S	Q	X	E	E
U	U	T	R	P	R	A	N	C	E	R	N	S
D	M	J	G	F	S	Q	S	D	U	V	C	G
O	N	D	J	Y	G	D	W	F	D	P	C	M
L	H	U	A	H	J	G	D	S	A	S	I	N
P	F	Y	W	N	Y	T	R	W	D	D	V	D
H	S	T	D	D	C	O	M	E	T	F	D	E
I	J	E	F	E	S	E	C	V	S	D	F	S
Y	D	O	N	N	E	R	R	H	Y	T	E	D
R	Q	D	S	A	B	G	J	T	F	S	E	F

ON THIS DAY

1642 New Zealand was first sighted by Dutch navigator Abel Tasman.

Taylor Swift, Dick Van Dyke and Jamie Foxx were all born on **December 13**.

DID YOU KNOW?!

In Japan, it's a tradition to eat **KFC** on Christmas Day. Orders have to be placed two months in advance!

Where do polar bears go to vote?

— *The North Poll!*

QUIZ TIME!

1 What sport used to be played on Boxing Day before it was banned?

2 What gifts did the Three Wise Men take to baby Jesus?

3 What type of Christmas did Elvis have?

ON THIS DAY

1799 George Washington, the first president of the USA, died.

King George VI, Shirley Jackson and Nostradamus were all born on **December 14.**

DID YOU KNOW?!

It only took six weeks for Charles Dickens to write **A Christmas Carol**.

What's worse than Rudolph with a runny nose?

— Frosty the Snowman with a hot flush!

QUIZ TIME!

1. In the UK, what fruit do children traditionally get in their stockings?

2. How many candles should go on an advent wreath?

3. What was the name of Scrooge's dead business partner?

Spot The Difference

One scene is not like the other! Can you spot **TEN** differences?

ON THIS DAY

1939   The movie *Gone With the Wind* premiered in Atlanta.

Gustave Eiffel, Nero and Michael King were all born on **December 15.**

DID YOU KNOW?!

The X in **X-Mas** is not an abbreviation. It actually stands for **"Chi"**, meaning Christ in Greek.

What did Adam say on the day before Christmas?

— *It's Christmas, Eve!*

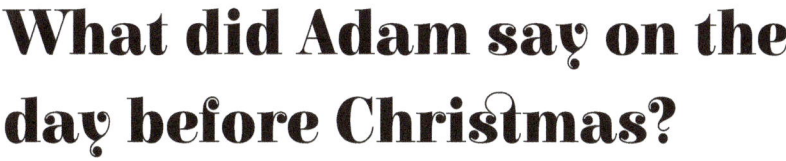

QUIZ TIME!

1. Where did the tradition of eating turkey on Christmas Day come from?

2. What star sign are you if you're born on Christmas Day?

3. Which country is the largest exporter of Christmas trees?

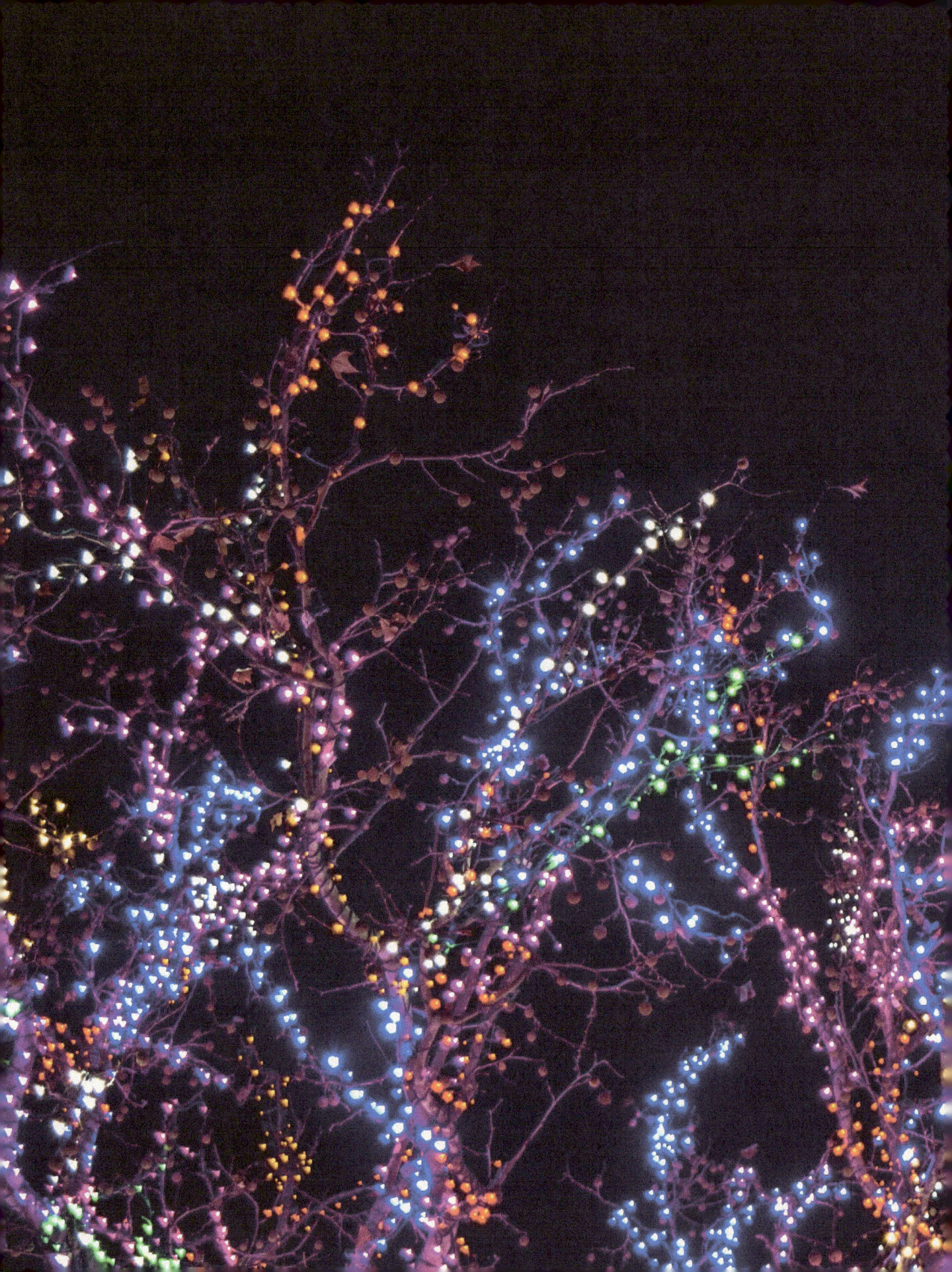

ON THIS DAY

1773 — Protesters protested the British tax on tea, better known as the *Boston Tea Party*.

Ludwig Van Beethoven, Jane Austen and Arthur C. Clarke were all born on **December 16.**

DID YOU KNOW?!

On December 16, 1965, **Jingle Bells** became the first song ever played in space.

Where do Santa's reindeers like to stop for lunch?

— Deery Queen!

QUIZ TIME!

1. Which popular Christmas decoration was named after the French word "estincelle" meaning spark?

2. What is Santa Claus called in France?

3. What is the capital of Christmas Island?

Crazy Christmas Crossword

Fill in the crossword puzzle using the clues below.

Across

3. Sharp Christmas plant
5. Fall from the sky
8. How Santa gets in
9. Famous snowman
10. Santa's tiny helpers
12. Red-Nosed Reindeer
14. Kris ___
15. Baby's bed

Down

1. Striped sweet
2. Given at Christmas
4. Rings out from churches
6. Colour of Santas beard
7. Bright celestial body
11. Hung over the fireplace
13. Santa's transport

ON THIS DAY

1903 The Wright brothers made the first ever successful flight in an airplane in North Carolina.

Pope Francis, Milla Jokovich and Manny Pacquiao were all born on **December 17.**

DID YOU KNOW?!

Between 1659 and 1681, **Christmas was illegal** in the United States' colonies. Oklahoma was the last U.S. state to declare Christmas a legal Holiday, in 1907.

What type of bread do elves eat?

— *Shortbread!*

QUIZ TIME!

1. What colour are mistletoe berries?

2. In which country is Santa Claus known as Babbo Natale?

3. How many tips does a snowflake have?

ON THIS DAY

1865 — Slavery was abolished in the United States.

Billie Eilish, Steven Spielberg and Franz Ferdinand were all born on **December 18.**

DID YOU KNOW?!

Bing Crosby's version of **White Christmas** is the highest-selling single of all time.

What do you get if you cross Santa Claus with a detective?

— *Santa Clues.*

QUIZ TIME!

1. Which US president banned Christmas trees from the White House?

2. In which novel is it *'always winter but never Christmas'*?

3. What would you be drinking if you had 'Glühwein'?

Chsritams
Word Scramble

Oh dear, Santa's having a bad day and he's gotten all his deliveries mixed up!

Can you unscramble these **country names** to give him a hand?

1. DAENLGN

2. SLRATAUAI

3. DCAANA

4. EXOCIM

5. EYARGNM

6. INSAP

7. IACHN

ON THIS DAY

1843 — Charles Dickens' *A Christmas Carol* was published.

Jake Gyllenhaal, Alyssa Milano and Reggie White were all born on **December 19.**

DID YOU KNOW?!

The first US president to put up an official **White House Christmas tree** was Franklin Pierce in the 1850s.

What do you sing on a snowman's birthday?

— *Freeze a jolly good fellow.*

QUIZ TIME!

1. What's the most popular type of tree to use as a Christmas tree?

2. Which US president had his own special eggnog recipe?

3. Who invented Christmas lights?

20

ON THIS DAY

1946 — *It's a Wonderful Life*, a classic holiday movie, premiered.

Dick Wolf, Dylan Wang and Kylian Mbappé were all born on **December 20.**

DID YOU KNOW?!

During the early 1900s, **Christmas lights** were seen as a status symbol as they were so expensive.

Who gives presents to baby sharks?

— Santa Jaws!

QUIZ TIME!

1 What real life person is Santa Claus based on?

2 What did the reindeers not let Rudolph do because of his red, shiny nose?

3 What percentage of Americans buy artificial Christmas trees?

What am I?

Use the guides below to colour in the grid on the right and discover the hidden picture.

1. (blue)
2. (light blue)
3. (black)
4. (brown)
5. (orange)
6. (light orange)
7. (dark brown)

2	2	2	2	2	2	1	2	2	2	2	2	2
2	1	2	7	7	2	2	2	7	7	2	1	2
2	2	7	2	7	7		7	7	2	7	2	2
2	2	2	7	7	2	5	2	7	7	2	2	2
2	1	2	2	7	5	5	5	7	2	2	1	2
2	2	2	2						2	2	2	2
2	2	4	4	4	4	4	4	4	4	4	2	2
2	4	6	6	4	4	4	4	4	6	6	4	2
2	2	2	2	4	4	4	4	4	2	2	2	2
1	2	2	2	3	4	4	4	3	2	2	2	1
2	2	2	2	4	4	4	4	4	2	2	2	2
2	2	1	2	4	4	6	4	4	2	1	2	2
2	2	2	2	2	4	4	4	2	2	2	2	2
2	1	2	2	2	2	2	2	2	2	2	1	2

21

ON THIS DAY

2012 — Psy's music video for *Gangnam Style* became the first to reach 1 billion views on YouTube.

Benjamin Disraeli, Jane Fonda and Emmanuel Macron were all born on **December 21.**

DID YOU KNOW?!

The best-selling Christmas toy in 1980 was a **Rubik's cube**, which cost $1.99. It now retails for over $10 (£9).

What did the monkey sing on Christmas Day?

— Jungle Bells.

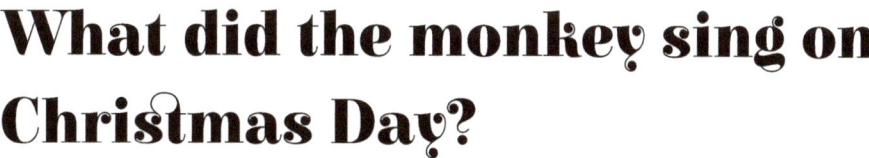

QUIZ TIME!

1. What does Santa say at the end of *A Visit from St. Nicholas* book?

2. What popular Christmas decoration is actually a parasitic plant?

3. Donald Trump makes a cameo appearance in which Christmas film?

22

ON THIS DAY

1989 Berlin's Brandenburg Gate reopened after the reunification of Germany.

Frank Kellogg, Maurice & Robb Gibb and Ralph Fiennes were all born on **December 22.**

DID YOU KNOW?!

The candy cane was invented in Germany in **1670**, when a choirmaster handed out sugar sticks to his choirboys to keep them quiet. However, after complaints from the church that they weren't religious enough, he bent them to look like a **shepherd's staff**.

What did the cow get for Christmas?

— *A cow-culator.*

QUIZ TIME!

1. In the holiday movie *It's A Wonderful Life*, what happened every time a bell rang?

2. What cartoon do Swedes traditionally watch on Christmas Eve?

3. What does Noel mean in Latin?

Santa's Speedy Sudoku

Aim of the game: fill in the blanks using the items below. Every item should only appear once in every row, column and 2x2 sub-grid.

But wait, it's not that easy! Everyone in the family has to take a go, and the fastest to solve it, wins!

23

ON THIS DAY

1888 — Vincent Van Gogh cut off his left ear after an argument with fellow artist Paul Gauguin.

Joseph Smith, Madam C. J. Walker and Bill Rodgers were all born on **December 23.**

DID YOU KNOW?!

Eggnog was first created and enjoyed by **Medieval monks** in the 13th century. They also added figs to the recipe.

What type of motorbike does Santa Claus ride?

— *A Holly Davidson!*

QUIZ TIME!

1   Who sang *"God bless us, everyone"*?

2   What were Frosty the Snowman's last words?

3   Which town in Florida keeps a decorated tree up all year round?

24

ON THIS DAY

1818 The Christmas carol *Silent Night* was first sung at a church in Austria.

Ricky Martin, Anthony Fauci and Howard Hughes were all born on **December 24.**

DID YOU KNOW?!

The most recorded Christmas song is **Silent Night**. Over 733 versions of the song have been copyrighted since 1978.

What do snowmen wear on their heads?

— *Ice caps!*

QUIZ TIME!

1. What is the main ingredient in gingerbread cookies? Flour, molasses or ginger?

2. What was the most popular toy of 1984?

3. In which year did the Elf on the Shelf tradition start?

Christmas Eve Double Word Puzzle

Let's challenge those brains before the big day tomorrow.

Unscramble the following list of shuffled words to solve the message at the end!

KBSEAT □□□□□■
                11

YUNNB □□□□□

TECROEAD □□□■□□■
              3   17

EGSG □□□□

RSSGA □■□□■
         4   10

HNUT □□□□

ENAEBJYLSL □□□□■□□■□□
                    5   13

CLCATHEOO □■□■□□□□■
              7   6   2

WROSLFE □□□□■■■
                    15 8 14

M											I		M			V		!
1	2	3	4	5	6	7	8	9	10	11	12	13	14	15	16	17	18

Happy 25 Christmas

ON THIS DAY

221 This date was first identified as the date of Jesus' birth by Sextus Julius Africanus.

Isaac Newton, Humphrey Bogart and Justin Trudeau were all born on **December 25.**

DID YOU KNOW?!

Around 15,000 Americans end up in the ER each year from **holiday-related decorating accidents.** Be safe! :)

Who hides in the bakery at Christmas?

— *A mince spy.*

QUIZ TIME!

1 During the holiday season what Christmas image does McDonalds put on its takeaway bags?

2 When was the first Starbucks Pumpkin Spice Latte launched?

3 What colour is Santa's belt?

Quiz Answers

Day 1
1. A flocked Christmas tree
2. Poinsettia
3. Hansel and Gretel

Day 2
1. Ebenezer
2. Macy's
3. Swans a-swimming

Day 3
1. A button
2. Eggnog
3. Bethlehem

Day 4
1. In 1843
2. Die Hard
3. Turkey

Day 5
1. Tom Hanks
2. England
3. Randy

Day 6
1. Treat every day like Christmas
2. Home Alone
3. Feliz Navidad

Day 7
1. Dasher, Dancer and Donner
2. Jingle Bells
3. He hides in Santa's sack.

Day 8
1. Germany
2. Someone special
3. Ikea

Day 9
1. Red wine, sugar and spices
2. Australia
3. Robin

Day 10
1. Donner (which is German for Thunder)
2. Robbie the Reindeer
3. A bowl full of jelly

Day 11
1. Cookies and milk
2. January 6th, also known as Three Kings Day.
3. Twice
4. Paris

Day 12
1. Paris
2. Jim Carrey
3. United Kingdom

Day 13
1. Fox Hunting
2. Gold, frankincense, and myrrh
3. A blue Christmas

Day 14
1. Tangerines
2. Four
3. Jacob Marley

Day 15
1. North America
2. Capricorn
3. Canada

Day 16
1. Tinsel
2. Père Noël
3. Settlement

Day 17
1. White
2. Italy
3. Six

Day 18
1. Theodore Roosevelt
2. The Lion, The Witch, and The Wardrobe, by C.S. Lewis
3. Mulled wine. The word is German.

Day 19
1. A Nordmann Fir
2. George Washington
3. Thomas Edison in 1880

Day 20
1. The Christian bishop St. Nicholas.
2. Join in any reindeer games.
3. Around 80%

Day 21
1. "Happy Christmas to all, and to all a good night!"
2. Mistletoe
3. Home Alone 2

Day 22
1. An angel gets their wings.
2. Donald Duck
3. Birth

Day 23
1. Andrea Bocelli.
2. I'll be back again someday.
3. Christmas, Florida.

Day 24
1. Flour
2. The Cabbage Patch Kids
3. 2005

Day 25
1. Trees
2. Fall 2004
3. Black

Game Solutions

Day 2 - Festive Food

				S	T	U	F	F	I	N	G	
	E	G	G	N	O	G						
		I									S	
C	A	N	D	Y	C	A	N	E			U	
O		G									G	
O		E									A	
K	F	R	U	I	T	C	A	K	E		R	
I		B	T			R					P	
E		R	U			I					L	
S		E		R		F					U	
		A			K		L				M	
		D	M	I	N	C	E	P	I	E	S	
						Y						
	T	A	N	G	E	R	I	N	E			

Day 4 - Gingerbread Maze

Day 8 - Feeling Merry and Musical

1. look down where he lay; Away in a Manger
2. and blowing; Jingle Bell Rock
3. corn; Let it Snow
4. near to us; Have Yourself a Merry Little Christmas
5. pipe, nose, coal; Frosty the Snowman
6. bad or good; Santa Claus is Coming to Town
7. night, shepherd; Silent Night
8. pumpkin; Rockin' Around the Christmas Tree

Day 12 - Reindeer Games

	B	L	I	T	Z	E	R		V	
									I	
	D	A	S	H	E	R			X	
R									E	
U			P	R	A	N	C	E	R	N
D						U				
O		D						P		
L		A						I		
P			N							D
H				C	O	M	E	T		
					E					
	D	O	N	N	E	R	R			

Day 14 — Spot the Difference

Day 16 - Crazy Christmas Crossword

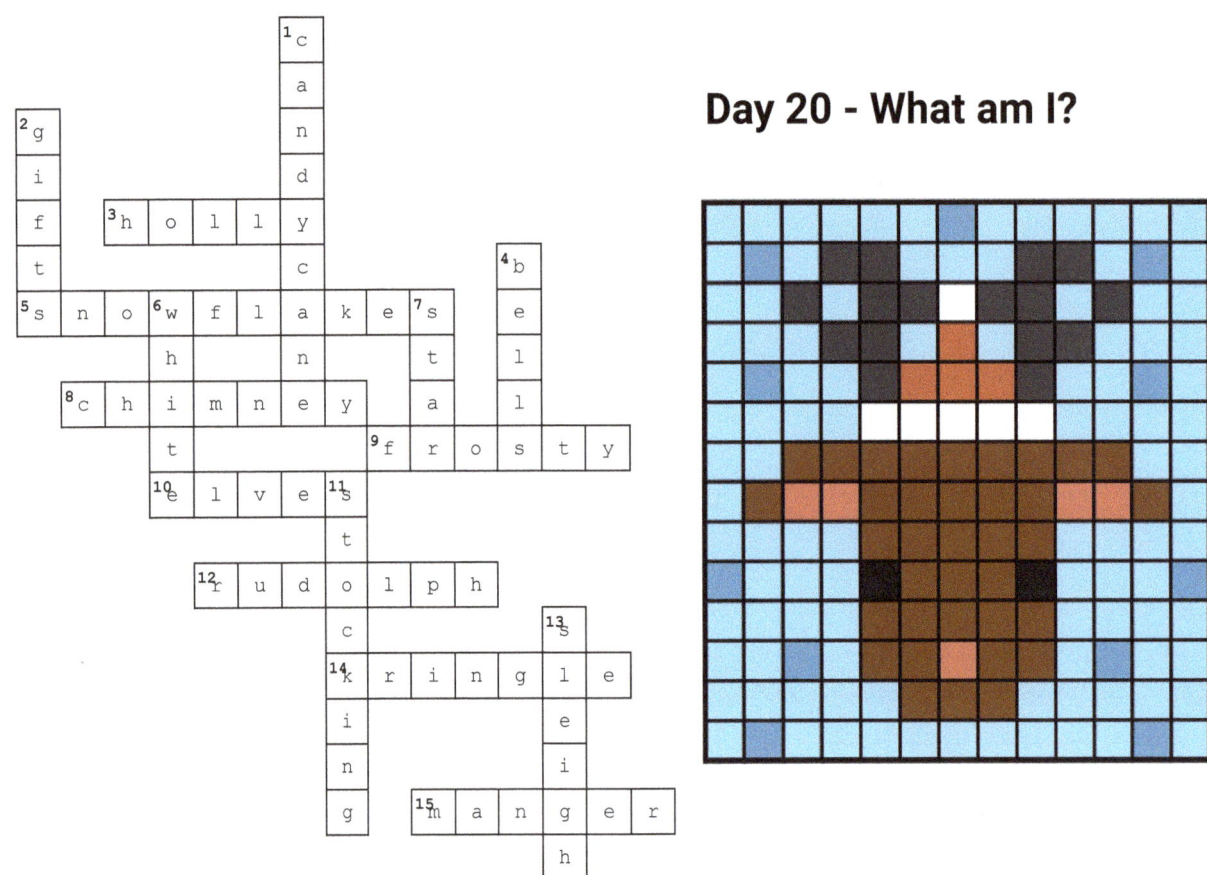

Day 20 - What am I?

Day 18 — Word Scramble
1. England
2. Australia
3. Canada
4. Mexico
5. Germany
6. Spain
7. China

Day 22 - Santa's Speedy Sudoku

Day 24 - Christmas Eve Double Puzzle

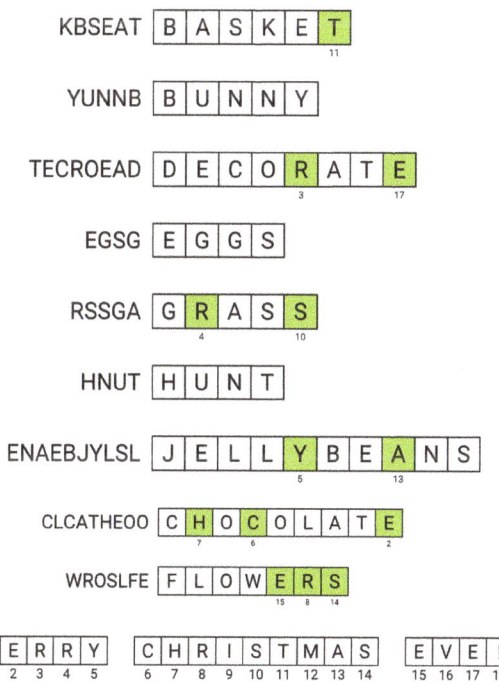

Competition time!

Did you spot our cute little elves throughout the book?!

Count how many you can find and enter your answer at:

www.bellanovabooks.com/christmascomp

You'll go in the draw to win **TWO FREE BOOKS**.

Good luck!

And that's all folks!

Wishing you the merriest of Christmases and the happiest of New Years.

You know what would make my Christmas? **A review from my beloved readers**! If you loved this book, please consider leaving a review. It really does make a difference; especially as it means I can bring out volume 2 of this book next year :)

www.ingramcontent.com/pod-product-compliance
Lightning Source LLC
LaVergne TN
LVHW070205080526
838202LV00063B/6562